WHAT IS A WALL, AFTER ALL?

Judy Allen

illustrated by Alan Baron

WALKER BOOKS
AND SUBSIDIARIES
LONDON · BOSTON · SYDNEY · AUCKLAND

Wherever you are when you open this book,

I bet you can see a wall if you look.

5

Could you build a wall?
No problem at all!
Put brick on brick.

Mortar makes
them stick.
Neat and slick.

It's a weak wall, a sick wall,
a leaning-on-a-stick wall,
a feeble wall, a quaky wall,
a crumbly, tumbly, shaky wall.

Keep it
straight.

That looks
great!

Oh,
but
wait…

Send for the strong crane
with the ball and long chain,
to bash it and smash it
and crash it down again!

A drystone wall is cleverly made.
Every stone is carefully laid.
Each shape has been picked to fit its own space,
so the wall stands firm on a solid base.

The walls of castles are built of blocks –
large blocks, stone blocks, cut out of rocks.
They are nearly square and almost neat
and mortar joins them where they meet.

9

There are walls made of glass
that shine in the sun,
and rubbery walls
that are silly – but fun!

There are brick walls and thick walls
and walls owned by cats,
and deep underground
there are cave walls, with bats.

11

There are tall walls, high walls,
climb up to the sky walls…
and little, low, short walls
that creep along the ground.

There are big, long, wide walls,
we've-got-something-to-hide walls,
and the walls of a lighthouse
that have to be round.

13

There are walls that are horribly fierce,
and walls that are terribly old.

There are walls that are meant to get hot,
and walls that ought to stay cold.

Some walls are there
to shut out invaders
(a safe keeps out robbers,
a fort keeps out raiders).

Others are different –
they're there to shut in.
(Think of people in prison,
or beans in a tin!)

Here is a wall that has to be tough
so it won't collapse when the weather gets rough,
and the wind is wild and the waves pound hard
and the stormy seas try to break through its guard.

There are two walls that are long, strong and round:
they're the walls of a tunnel that runs underground.
The wall of a dam has to stand like a rock
to hold back the river whose path it must block.

Most indoor walls are plain and flat,

till smartened up with this and that.

If you sit on a wall
you may not be alone…

small things could be living
in cracks in the stone.

If you want to climb a mountain wall you will probably need stout boots and crampons and warm clothing and pegs to hammer into narrow cracks and wedges to hammer into wide cracks and a peg hammer to put them in with and an ice axe and a hammer axe (which is a short ice axe) and a strong rope and a hard hat.

Hard h

Karabiner

Strong rope

Pegs

Crampons

Tape sling

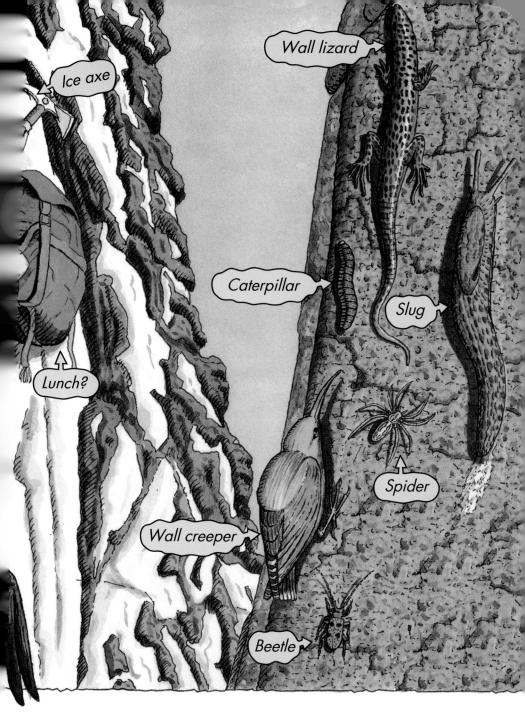

But others can climb without all that.

Where are you? In a room? In a garden?
In a car? A bus? A train?
In a field? On a boat?
Maybe up in a plane?
In the street? On the beach?
In a hot-air balloon?

In a café? In bed?
Perhaps on the moon?
Well, wherever you are
when you finish this book,
I bet you can see
a wall, if you look.

Do you know?

… why a drystone wall is called a drystone wall? It's because the stones are not held together with putty or mortar. Look at the picture on page 8. You can see that

each stone has been put in just the right place so the wall will stand firm and strong with the stones perfectly balanced.

… what "dressing" stones means? It means cutting and shaping them. The man in the green hat on page 9 is dressing a stone for the castle wall.

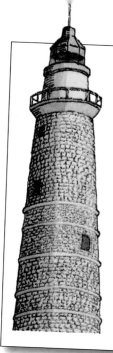

… why the walls of a lighthouse have to be round? Lighthouses stand on the edge of cliffs or on rocks in the sea, where their light can warn and guide ships when it's dark. They are shaped so the strong sea winds slide around them and don't push them over.

… what pebble-dash is? It's a decoration for outside walls. A mixture of sand and cement is spread over the wall. Then pebbles are thrown – or dashed – against it so they stick. No one puts pebble-dash indoors – except the man on page 21.

… that the rooms of castles often had tapestries on their walls? Tapestries are huge pieces of fabric with pictures sewn on them. They covered the cold stone walls and made the rooms warmer.

… that there are walls on the moon – but they are not made by people. They are the walls of craters, colliding with the moon's surface.

... that the Great Wall of China is 2400 kilometres long? Some people say it can be seen from the moon, but they are wrong. It can be photographed from satellites though.

... what the dam wall on page 19 is for? It's blocking the river to collect water. Pipes take the water to taps in homes and factories. The force of the water flowing through the dam can be used to create electricity.

Kinds of bricks

Walls can be built of almost anything, but often they are built of stone, which is natural, or man-made bricks.

People have been making bricks with clay for about 10,000 years. Once they were baked hard in the sun. Now they are baked in an oven called a kiln.

Building blocks cut from stone or rock are often called bricks when they are brick-shaped.

Mortar is the stuff that sticks the bricks together. Today, mortar is usually made of cement.

Bricks may be named for what they are used for. The top line of bricks in a wall is called coping, so that is where the *saddleback coping* brick and the *half round coping* brick would be set.

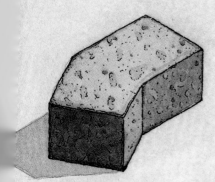

Dogleg brick

Bevelled bat brick

Plinth squint brick

Half round
coping brick

Limestone sneck

Decorative brick

Bricks may be named for what they are made of. Limestone, sandstone, marble and granite are different kinds of rock that can be shaped into building bricks.

Sandstone

Bricks may be named for their shapes. Look at the *birdsmouth* and the *dogleg*.

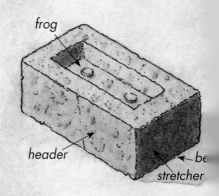

frog

header

be

stretcher

The parts of bricks

Be careful about climbing on walls — whatever they are made of — remember what happened to Humpty Dumpty!

Marble

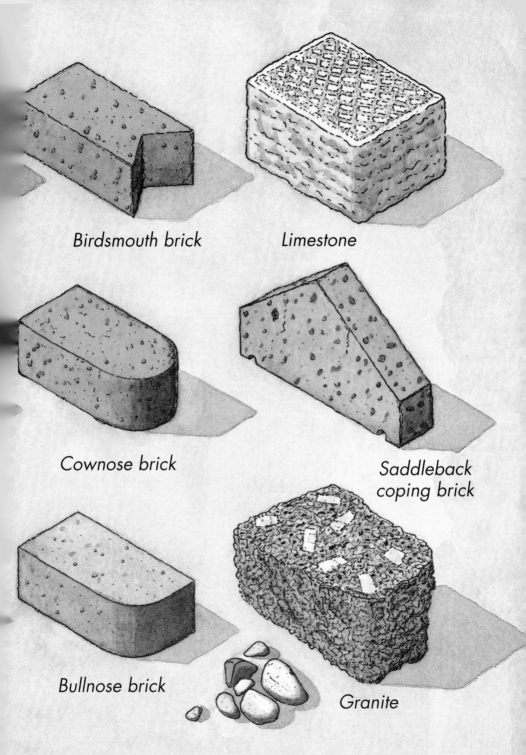

Birdsmouth brick

Limestone

Cownose brick

Saddleback coping brick

Bullnose brick

Granite

35

Index

About the Author

Judy Allen got the idea for this book
when she was watching a television
programme about a wall that divided
a country. "I was watching this horrible
wall being pulled down," she says,
"and after that I was amazed at how
many different kinds of wall
I could think of without even trying.
I decided there was a book in
there somewhere!"

About the Illustrator

Alan Baron says, "I once built a wall.
It was to be 23cm thick. As the
wall grew, it got thicker and thicker.
At 90cm high the wall was 28cm thick.
I wasn't very good at it.
Then I improved. At 1.8m high
the wall was back to 23cm thick.
To this day the wall has a great big bulge
in the middle. No one knows why.
Except me."

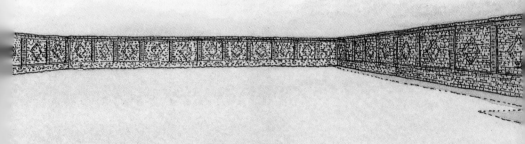

There are 10 titles in the BETTWS
5-7-18

READ AND DISCOVER series.

Which ones have you read?

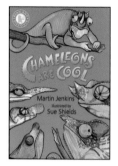
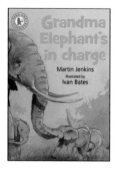
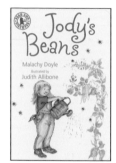

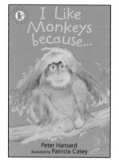

Available from all good booksellers